Hind's Feet in the Making

"Looking unto Jesus"
Zelma R Cowan

Hind's Feet in the Making

Zelma Ruth Cowan

All scriptures are from the King James Version of the Holy Bible unless otherwise noted.

Printed in the United States

Publishing services by Selah Publishing Group, LLC, Arizona. The views expressed or implied in this work do not necessarily reflect those of Selah Publishing Group.

ISBN: 1-58930-082-3
Library of Congress Control Number: 2002117229

"The Lord God is my strength,
my personal bravery
and my invincible army;
He makes my feet like hinds' feet,
and will make me to walk,
[not to stand still in terror, but to walk]
and make spiritual
progress upon my high places
[of trouble, suffering or responsibility]!"
Habakkuk 3:19 Amplified Bible

Dedication

My heart is overwhelmed and indeed grateful for all the following individuals and organizations that have had such a vital part in my life, making it so special in the Lord:

Christian parents, who guided me in the ways of the Lord;

A solid church, faithful in directing me into the word of God;

A Bible college, that grounded me in the word of God and followed me with its prayers;

A missionary family, which has been a constant encouragement and blessing to work with and has been faithful in prayers, too;

A host of friends, who have been faithful to pray and support me along my life's journey.

To all of these, I dedicate this book praying it will be used for His honor and glory.

Table Of Contents

Foreword

In 1976, Mrs. Helen Baugh assigned me to work with Zelma Cowan, because she had been working alone and her health was not great. At that time I had never met her, but excitement filled my entire being. Now I understand why. From the first day till the present, it has been a joy to be able to see "Jesus in action" in her practical every day living.

This book reveals how God does not require riches or fame to get His work done. He is looking for committed souls who want to do His will above everything else, no matter what. Zelma was one of those who was willing to go to out of the way places as He led her. Your heart will be touched as you read her experiences of learning to have hinds' feet. She was not looking for riches or rewards; but was living a life of obedient service, so that, on that day when she stands before the Judge of the whole world, her reward will be to hear Him say, "Well done, thou good and faithful servant."

Betty Edwards

Acknowledgements

Title page picture was taken by Jean Scott at Ecola Park, near Cannon Beach, Oregon.

All editing and typing were done by my partner, Betty Edwards. Computer work was done by Rick Salas.

Introduction

Have you ever stopped to take a good look at your feet? Yes, when a baby is born, the parents are anxious to check out that tiny bundle, especially those little hands and feet. They are so precious! And it is a relief to find all those little fingers and toes are perfect!

Corie and Kelly Kiker, Zelma's twin grand nieces, with lots of fingers and toes to check!

After much to-do, we soon forget about them until they begin to stub these dear little toes. Oh, does that ever hurt! The tears flow and so much understanding and love are needed!

Isn't it wonderful that we have a loving God who is concerned about our feet? Every time we trip, stumble, or even stub our toes, He is there for us, to comfort and understand. Yes, He even wants to make our feet like hinds' feet! A hind is a young deer, gazelle, or hart— a sure-footed beast. I understand that the hinds' feet are so well coordinated that their hind feet step right into the tracks of their front feet, therefore enabling them to go into the most narrow places without calamity. *"He makes my feet like the hinds' [firm and able]; He sets me secure and confident upon the heights."* II Samuel 22:34 AMP The Psalmist puts it this way, *"He makes my feet like hinds' feet [able to stand firmly or make progress on the dangerous heights of testing and trouble]; He sets me securely upon my high places."* Psalm 18:33 AMP.

Our feet may not be much to look at and admire as we grow up, but how important they are to our well being, physically and spiritually. Many times we find references to our feet in the Bible, God's Holy Word. Our feet are very important to Him.

"Ponder the paths of thy feet, and let all thy ways be established. Turn not to the right hand not to the left: remove thy foot from evil." Proverbs 4:26,27 KJV How thankful I am that the Almighty God is concerned and interested in every step I take. His help and guidance is always there for me.

CHAPTER 1

The Starting Point

September second was the big date in a little place called Boyd's Creek, Tennessee, where a baby girl was born into the Cowan family. She joined a sister Wanda, a brother William (who was better known as Bill), and another sister Dora Lee.

The Cowan family

I did not know that before I was born my parents had prayed, dedicating me to the Lord for full time Christian service. Neither did I know that my name, Zelma, means "Divinely Protected." These facts became known to me a short time ago, before I started writing this book. As I reflect upon my life, His divine protection has become very real to me, and my parent's dedication of me became a reality.

Our family stayed in Tennessee until I was six months old, at which time we moved to Riverside, California. Since my parents were dedicated Christians, we started attending Sunday school and church right away. I was enrolled in the cradle role department. What a special treat to have a family who attended church together!

Later a baby boy was born into our family. His name was Charles. I think of him, Chuck, as the family clown, because he brought many laughs to our family. I remember

Chuck with the family dog, Chubby

at meal time when it was Chuck's turn to ask the blessing, "give us this day our daily bread," was heartfelt. You see, he was thankful for every kind of bread he could think of. Sometimes his prayer became rather lengthy. All my brothers and sisters were very special to me and I thank God for my wonderful family. At the time of this writing, all my family, except my sister Dora Lee, have gone home to be with the Lord.

I also had a great church family. The pastor, an outstanding man of God, served at this church for twenty-six years. Despite the fact that the church was large, he still had time to talk with the children and young people, making them feel very special. My parents felt we should show him respect and call him Doctor Catherwood, but he insisted that we call him Uncle Willie. This man of God had a tremendous impact on my life.

I was also blessed with some wonderful Sunday school teachers who taught the Word of God faithfully, turning my thoughts toward God. The youth pastors were always there to encourage me during those teen years when help was always needed. It would be impossible to list the multitude of individuals that God has used in my life as my feet were being made like hinds' feet.

My heart is full and overflowing with gratitude for each one, knowing that God will reward them all for their faithfulness. Many of these dear people have gone home to their rewards. My parents both lived to see their prayers of dedication answered. How grateful I am for that!

CHAPTER 2

Crucial Giant Steps Taken

Because of God's faithfulness in giving me such good Christian training, it is no wonder that at an early age I became aware of God and his love for me. All of the Bible verses I learned in Sunday school began to prepare me for the biggest and most important step I would ever take in my life.

"For all have sinned and come short of the glory of God," Romans 6:23 KJV was one of these verses. That little word "all" haunted me. It was a nice, warm day and I was out doors playing, when all of a sudden our bantam rooster started fighting our bantam hen, which really scared me. This was true violence in those days. I called my mother to the scene for help. She picked up a little stick and threw it at them, in hopes of breaking up the fight. That little stick hit the rooster in the head and he toppled over dead into a small pond we had for our ducks. Romans 6:23 came to mind. *"The wages of sin is death."* Pay day had come! How often God uses the simple little things and incidents to remind us of all our great needs. Questions popped into my mind and heart. How about the fights I had with my sisters and brothers? Was I a sinner? That little word "all" must include me!

It was soon after that incident and reminder that I took that big step. I asked the Lord Jesus to come into my heart and life. I wanted to be forgiven and cleansed from all my sin, and I needed His help to live for Him. *"But the gift of*

God is eternal life through Jesus Christ our Lord." Romans 6:23 KJV Now I had it! I had just taken that giant step! At the age of eight, I did not understand all that had taken place in my life, but I was one excited little girl!

Alicia Fletcher, Zelma's great grand neice.
Is she prepared for the crucial, giant step?

One afternoon my aunt and uncle came to visit us. I was so anxious to tell them about becoming a Christian that I ran and jumped on the running board of the car before my uncle had a chance to stop. I received a good lecture about that. However, they were happy to hear about my big decision.

The next few years, I was to learn that the Christian life was full of ups and downs. The growing pains were for sure. I also learned that God's love and understanding was always with me. Junior high and high school seemed to be the most difficult. How clumsy my Christian life was! I felt like the proverbial "bull in a china closet." My feet were far from being like hinds' feet.

In preparation for that giant step, Zelma went to Sunday School and church. The Bible verses put to memory in those days prepared her for that big step.

Our church had summer camps for the young people and I was thrilled when I could go. It was at one of those camps that an overwhelming conviction came over me that God wanted all of me, even for Christian service. I could not rest until I said "yes" to God. I did not know where or how He would use me, or even if He could use me. I was just a weak, bashful, awkward teenager, still trying to get my life together.

God in His infinite wisdom and plan already had started preparing me for full time Christian service. He began by putting me into paths of service. First, I was asked to help with a Sunday school class. I really liked working with the pre-school children because they were so sweet and excited about learning. My next path of service was to teach a primary class at the Spanish mission. This was a work our church sponsored and my father was the teacher for the teenagers. It was nice to share in this ministry with him and it was quite a challenge! My senior year in high school was filled with the many questions that we all face at that age. The big question had already been settled and I knew my next step was to decide upon a college that would give me the special training I would need to prepare for His service. The choice of a Bible school was no problem. About that time, Doctor John Mitchell had held a Bible conference in our church and after hearing him expound the Scriptures for a week, I knew Multnomah School of the Bible was the place for me. After praying much, my application was sent and my acceptance was received . I was one happy girl!

However there was another big step I would need to take—a step of faith. My family was unable to help me out financially, so I would need to get a job and work my way through school. I worked at many different jobs. Some I enjoyed, some I did not. I had to learn that each job was a gift from God, and therefore very important.

I worked in a dog food factory, did lots of babysitting, house cleaning, and ironing. For a while I worked in a jewelry store. The main job was working in a public school with handicapped children. I loved this work and found the teachers and other workers a real blessing in many ways. Each year when I returned to school, I was invited to come back and work. It was a real learning experience for me in preparing me for His service.

While attending Bible school we were given different assignments for Christian service.

First, I had a Sunday school class of eighth graders, which was thrilling and an awesome responsibility. Later, I was assigned to a "Real Life Club" which was for young people.

This assignment was very interesting and challenging since several in this group were deaf. We learned to communicate and some of them even learned how to sing a pretty good tune.

The most exciting assignment I had was to go with a team of girls to a detention home for girls. Each Sunday night, we would conduct a service. Following the service, we were able to talk with the girls and answer their questions. As time passed, I found myself the leader of the team and the doors to this ministry began to open wider. One Sunday night after the service, I was asked by the headmistress if I could come out on Thursday nights, bring one of the faculty members, and conduct a Bible study. Miss Helen Carlson was willing to go with me; she presented the Bible study and I led the singing. Watching her give the lesson in her own unique way was a genuine learning experience. We had some rare moments, but the blessings far exceeded the difficult times. I will never cease to be grateful for the Bible school training. I am quite sure that the faculty and staff spent much time on their knees praying me through school!

My schedule was filled with classes, study time, working as much as time would allow, plus extra activities such as Women's Council president and other assignments of service. It is amazing to think about it all. "*It is God who girdeth me with strength and maketh my way perfect. He maketh my feet like hinds' feet and setteth me upon my high places.*" Psalm 18:32, 33 KJV.

While working at the school for handicapped children, I developed a friendship with some of the teachers and other workers. One teacher, Edith Frie, a lovely Christian, became very special. She took an extraordinary interest in me and we had many times of good Christian fellowship together.

Zelma and Edith Frie at the school for the handicapped

One evening, she asked me to go as her guest to a Christian Business and Professional Women's Club dinner. I was excited and deeply impressed by the unique ministry of that organization. At that time, all my thoughts were about foreign missionary work, focusing primarily on China.

During the summer vacations, while attending school, I worked at Mount Hermon Conference Center. This provided extra finances for the following school year, as well as being involved in Christian service. The week of Youth Conference was priceless because I was allowed to leave my other responsibilities and be the counselor for the Chinese girls who came. That proved to be an unforgettable experience. Before I had finished my Bible school training, China was closed to missionary work. This was a big disappointment! As I prayed and talked with many missionaries, there was still the strong feeling that God was directing to the foreign field. But most of all, He just wanted my availability for whatever and wherever He wanted me to be.

During my senior year, I decided it was time to start making plans for the foreign field. After much prayer, applications were sent to two different mission boards. Whichever replied first would be the one to follow. Soon one responded and the preliminaries proceeded. All that was left to do was a physical exam. Because of my age, the mission board wanted me to wait till September to have the physical exam and finish the process. They felt that twenty-two years was a little too young.

That summer was very exciting, working at Mount Hermon, anticipating the time when final preparations would be made for going to a foreign mission field. The anticipation was overwhelming waiting for that event! And I felt really great! The examination turned out to be a big disappointment. My sinuses and allergy problems would not tolerate an extreme climate and different foods of a foreign country. The little phrase, "Disappointments are His Appointments," became very real to me. How did I miss God's will on this one? Had He misled me? There were great soul searchings, along with much frustration.

After finishing work at Mount Hermon that summer, I went home for some rest and to do some more praying for guidance. Yes, rest was a real need alright, but more than that, a greater need to *"be still, and know that I am God."* Psalm 46:10a KJV The Greek word for "still" is "relax." So the actual need was to learn how to relax in the Lord and to know that God was still in charge. I took my Bible and went to my room, determined to read until God gave some direction as to the next step. Starting in the book of Matthew, I read until chapter 9, verse35, which seemed to stand out. *"And Jesus went about all the cities and villages...."* My attention went back to that night when my friend, Edith Frie, had taken me to that dinner meeting, where they had told about the Stonecroft Ministries, which took the gospel to cities and villages—just like Jesus had done! That organization had a ministry that was geared to reach business women and homemakers in the cities and to send workers into rural areas and villages to open closed churches and start churches where there were none. It started with teams of girls known as Rural Missionaries. As the years passed, the work was turned over to men with families, who are now called Village Missionaries.

My heart leaped with excitement as I realized God was speaking to me about this ministry! A person did not need to go to a foreign country in order to be a missionary because the world is the field. Even Jesus did not neglect the cities and the villages. *"But when he saw the multitudes, he was moved with compassion on them, because they were faint and were scattered abroad, as sheep having no shepherd."* Matthew 9:36 KJV An awesome burden flooded my soul. This was a vivid picture of the needs in rural America and in the cities, too. The tears began to flow, recognizing there was such a mission field at my finger tips. The responsibility and mission were tremendous. *"The harvest truly is plenteous, but the labourers are few; Pray ye therefore the Lord of the harvest, that he will send forth labourers into his har-*

vest." Matthew 9: 37, 38 KJV. The prayer, "Here am I; send me," became a virtual reality in my life. Inexpressible joy and peace flooded my soul!

Soon I contacted my friend, Edith, and she was prompt to see that all the needed information was sent, including an application to enter the work. After this, events began to happen quickly. It was a memorable day when I received word I had been accepted as one of their Rural Missionaries!

The following poem based on Matthew 9 expresses what was in my heart when God spoke to me that day.

Sheep Without A Shepherd

Sheep without a shepherd, what a pitiful sight to see.
They wander here and there, not knowing where to flee.
When one is injured, sick or cold, there is no one
To carry them back to the fold.
If one should stray and become lost from the flock,
Again, there is no one to search around the clock.
When souls are without the Savior,
Their condition is the same.
They have no one to turn to, no one their souls to claim.
Yes, sheep without a shepherd is a frightful sight to see;
But souls without a Savior is a far worse degree!

CHAPTER 3

The Master Foot Physician

We are living in a time when it seems every one is specialized in something. This is true for doctors. When one has a physical problem, a primary care doctor sends him to a specialist for that problem. Now, the foot doctors have their specialties, too—toe nails, corns, bunions. After all, we do want the best!

As we consider the Master Foot Physician, we will find a Specialist that no one can top! All of the medical degrees in the world are nothing compared with His credentials!!

"He is the Lord God!" Habakkuk 3:19 AMP The One who created everything, is the One who created even our feet.

Each of us has the exact set of feet He carefully and masterfully planned for us. Because He is the all-wise and all-knowing God, He has a purpose and plan for each set of feet He created. If we were to talk to a podiatrist or any foot specialist, we would be fascinated to learn the unique differences in feet—some short, some long, some wide, some slender, some flat, some with very high arches. My feet were very different because they had extra bones in them. This, too, was part of God's plan we shall consider later.

Habakkuk also states that the Lord God, the Master Physician, is my strength. An awesome thought! He knew we would be weak and awkward individuals who would need His strength and power in order to walk and use our feet for His glory. Daily He infuses us with His strength. *"God is our refuge and strength, a very present help in trouble."*

Psalms 46:1 KJV *"And He said unto me, My grace is sufficient for thee; for my strength is made perfect in weakness."* II Corinthians 12:9 KJV Just think, when we are weak, His strength is made perfect!

Our verse also says, *"He is my personal bravery."* How wonderful to know HE is my personal bravery. When the going gets tough and all seems to be going wrong, He is there to stand in my stead. *"When the enemy shall come in like a flood, the Spirit of the Lord shall lift up a standard against him."* Isaiah 59:19b KJV God understands that we are as mere cowards, not knowing how to handle the big giants, with whom we are confronted in our daily walk *"The Lord is my light and my salvation; of whom shall I be afraid?"* Psalm 27:1 KJV

As we follow through in our verse, we find these astounding words: *"He is my invincible army."* Victory is sure! He is invincible! He will fight for us! All we need to do is to stop trying to fight our own battles and let the Lord fight for us. This is a very difficult lesson to learn and we need to review it over and over again. *"The Lord shall fight for you, and ye shall hold your peace."* Exodus 14:14 KJV This verse often speaks to me, as I realize the battles are all a part of my feet becoming like hinds' feet. A tremendous joy and comfort comes from knowing that *"the Lord is my strength, my personal bravery, and my invincible army"! "Thine, O Lord, is the greatness, and the power, and the glory, and the victory, and the majesty; for all that is in the heaven and in the earth is thine. Thine is the kingdom, O Lord, and thou art exalted as head above all. Both riches and honor come of thee, and thou reignest over all; and in thine hand is power and might; and in thine hand it is to make great, and to give strength unto all. Now therefore, our God, we thank thee, and praise thy glorious name."* I Chronicles 29:11-13.KJV

CHAPTER 4

Foot Conditions

We are confronted by many foot problems, which we would rather forget and go about our business. But somehow when that bunion, blister, or toenail problem shows up, we are faced with that constant nagging pain that just does not let us forget. Finally, we do something about it and find relief. We do not think our feet are all that important and so often fail to care for them as we should.

It has been thrilling for me to learn that God is interested in my feet. When He formed my feet He intended to keep them in good condition. It is also good to know He did not make a mistake, if our feet do not seem to be perfect in our sight.

All through my growing up years, I was plagued with pain in my feet and legs. I saw many doctors, and they seemed to think it was growing pains that I would outgrow. As I grew older, the doctors tried all the usual things for pain—exercise, medications. Nothing seemed to help.

It was on my first assignment with the Stonecroft Ministries that I had a very severe time of pain. I tried everything that had been done in the past and nothing seemed to work. One day while talking to a friend she told me about an outstanding doctor who, she was certain, could help me. It would take some time to get an appointment, but she would try her best to get one for me. After much prayer, the appointment became a reality.

He gave me a series of shots and then one day, he said, "You really need to get those extra bones removed from your feet before you end up in a wheel chair." He explained to me that the extra bones that I had since birth were pulling my legs inward, thereby wearing my hip sockets down. No wonder I had pain!! I was still getting over that shock when he told me that immediate surgery was necessary. He also said, "Go home and pray about it." That was a first! My first reaction was to stand stand still in terror. How often when a major decision is needed, we would rather stand still and do nothing. Habakkuk 3:19 says we are to "*walk and make spiritual progress.*"

I did go to prayer in earnest! The dollar signs kept popping up and my income stayed the same—eighty-seven dollars and fifty cents a month!! The Master Foot Physician gently reminded me that He was in charge and trustworthy. Here I was, a missionary, led by Him all the way, and was He going to fail me at that point? I did not think so.

At the next appointment with the doctor, arrangements were made for the surgery. The month long stay in the hospital was longer than expected, but some lessons in faith were destined to be learned. Learning to walk with these made-over feet was quite a chore. At the same time, I was learning some very real lessons in my walk of faith, so the Master Physician was working double time with me.

Not only did I find myself without pain for the first time in my life, but I was experiencing God's faithfulness in taking care of all those dollar signs. Before the bills came flooding in, the dollars did—enough for the entire bill! There was only one bill left and that would be a big one. When I went back to the doctor for my final checkup, I asked him about his bill and he just quoted a verse of scripture from the Bible: *"How beautiful are the feet of them that preach the gospel of peace and bring glad tidings of good things."* Romans 10:15 KJV Then he said, "There will be no bill. The least I can do is to keep those feet in shape!" My heart was humbled and overwhelmed, to say the least!

No wonder no more money had come in for the doctor bill!!

One of the big blessings was that God allowed me to share Christ with several people during that long stay in the hospital. I was able to correspond with some of them and keep up on their spiritual growth in faith. I found out that it is better to walk than to stand still—the only way to make spiritual progress. To walk can be painful at times, but very challenging. Most of all, it strengthened and increased my faith.

CHAPTER 5

Therapy That Brings Progress

I found a great deal of therapy was needed after my foot surgery, but even more was needed for my spiritual progress. Therapy must start out gradually, not too much at one time. God is so good to measure out the therapy at perfect intervals. As progress is made, we become stronger in faith and reliance on Him.

Now that my feet were strong enough to stand upon, it was time to walk and make some spiritual progress. Habakkuk 3:19 AMP says, *"but to walk and make [spiritual] progress upon my high places [of trouble, suffering or responsibility.]"* Yes, missionaries have troubles, suffering and responsibilities. At times it can be overwhelming! However, God wants to use all that comes our way to enhance our ministry and therefore to help those to whom we minister. At the same time we are strengthened.

In 1953, I arrived in a little community in eastern Oregon, where I was to start my rural missionary work with Jean Scott. The people there were unusually gracious and it did not take long to fall in love with that place and those lovely people.

I did not realize there would be so many adjustments to make in this new life as a missionary. Coping with the cold—sometimes below zero weather—was quite an adjustment, especially after having spent most of my life in the land of sunshine. I remember one winter night when it was ten below zero, our heating fuel ran out. We were mighty thankful to obtain a small amount of fuel, but it only lasted until midnight. The rest of that night we spent trying to keep pipes from freezing, by letting all the faucets

Zelma and Jean Scott

run slightly. We had all the little electric heaters running that we could find and that were not in use already. A big light bulb was put under the hood of the car to keep the engine from freezing, too. The fuel truck was a welcome sight the next morning. This was another high place of trouble.

It was early in my ministry, that I received word that my mother was very ill and not expected to live. I had never experienced losing a loved one before. Since it was in the dead of winter and the roads were icy, it was no surprise to hear that the bus would not be coming through our area. I prayed much, for the bus was the only way out of town. After making some phone calls, I soon had my ticket and was packed ready to go whenever it came. Much to everyone's surprise, the bus arrived that day and it was almost on time! When the driver was questioned about it, he said that he somehow felt he could make it, so came on anyhow, in spite of the report. We arrived in Portland as the bus to Los Angeles was just about ready to leave. Perfect timing! The Master Therapist was helping me through it all! *"Strengthened with all might, according to His glorious power, unto all patience and longsuffering with joyfulness; giving thanks unto the Father."* Colossians 1:11,12 KJV This verse was very real to me at that time.

High places started coming, one after another. Summer had arrived and it was just as hot as it had been cold. The time came for Jean's vacation and this would mean my being alone with all the responsibilities for a couple of weeks. The next Sunday arrived and I had worked hard to prepare for all the services. A dear lady came with her children. After her husband dropped them off, he went home, planning to pick them up after church, as he usually did. When he did not show, they hitched a ride home with their neighbor. On arriving home, they discovered he had died of a massive heart attack.

The community had its own phone company. The phones were the old wall, hand-crank type. Whenever there was an emergency, there was a long and steady ring. Upon receiving a call about his death, I had my own emergency. This would be my first funeral that I had ever conducted.

Questions came roaring in—what next? How? Why? When? The Lord God, my Master foot physician was there to calm me down. I began to pray for guidance and soon realized the first step was to go visit the family. They needed comfort and I needed information concerning their plans.

Since I had not yet acquired my driver's license and I was using my learner's permit, I decided to call our local sheriff, who was also a member of our church, to see if he could drive me over to see the family. He was very willing to help in any way he could. When he came, he said, "I'm going to let you drive to keep you in practice." Well, his car had a stick shift and I was learning on an automatic shift. He soon found out what a jerky ride he was about to encounter! We finally made it and I talked with the family to get all the information for the obituary and plans for the funeral. After a time of prayer with them, we were on our way home. The drive was a bit smoother now.

There were some questions that needed answers, so I decided to check Jean's files to see if she might have some notes from a funeral she had conducted. A plan was needed. To my surprise, Jean had taken all her notes with her to rearrange them. One thing for sure, I needed a little message, and God had already laid a verse of scripture on my heart, so I started working on it right away. "*Whereas ye know not what shall be on the next day. For what is your life? It is even a vapor, that appeareth for a little time, and then vanisheth away.*" James 4:14 KJV The Lord helped me through that evening service, tired as I was. The next morning, I was rested and assured that God would work out all the details of the funeral on Tuesday. God works often when we are not aware of it.

The day before this man had passed away, one of my Bible college teachers was in his office and became burdened for me. As he remembered, I had not taken the course for pastors, which he taught. This course contained all the information for conducting funerals. He was so concerned, he promptly sent me a set of his notes from his class, which arrived the day before the funeral. All the many questions were answered, and I was able to be well prepared for that funeral service.

The day of the funeral turned out to be very hot. The church was filled with flowers and I decided to open the windows on both sides of the platform, to try to alleviate my allergy problems. All went well, until I started with my little message. The wind came up and a huge gust of wind came through the windows, blowing all my notes off the pulpit, over the casket, and half way down the aisle! My full dependence had to be upon the Lord God. What a rare lesson I learned on this very high place of trouble. *"Faithful is he that calleth you, who also will do it."* I Thessalonians 5:24 KJV It was He who quickened my mind, bringing the message to my mind, and He did it for His glory!

A missionary must be prepared for any situation—to pray, to sing, to speak, or even die. I have been called upon to pray at many different functions, such as funerals, school events, graduations, and dedications (one time at a dedication of a big bank), senior citizen meetings, and the list goes on. I have also been called upon to sing in a duet, a trio, choirs, and even solos. The most difficult solo was for a precious, little two year old girl's funeral. She and her identical twin were in my Sunday school class

There are always requests for speaking here and there—worship services, Sunday school classes of all ages, children's classes, youth meetings, baccalaureate services, and school events of all kinds. I remember once I was asked to present the creation story to a high school class. I was amazed at how many had never heard of it before. One time at a Christian Women's Club, the speaker lost her voice suddenly, and I was asked to fill in on the spur of the moment. These are high places God allows us to tread upon, reminding us of His power and strength.

Oh, yes! I also found out that a missionary can face death, too. A family moved into our community and the mother and children came to church the first Sunday they were there. Of course, they were welcomed with opened arms. It did not take very long to recognize that their background was troubled and unhappy. Daily the wife and children would come to visit us and share another chapter in their unstable lives. We found the mother to be a fairly new Christian, eager to learn all she could. Her husband was far from being a Christian and became very agitated because the rest of the family was really interested in learning all they could about God and His ways. We were totally blessed as we watched them grow in the Lord.

One Sunday afternoon, the children came running to our house screaming, "Daddy's trying to kill us!" Shortly, the mother came following them. We let them in and locked the door and called the sheriff, who was not at home. We tried to comfort and quiet them as we prayed with them. We fixed something for them to eat and kept trying to call the sheriff. Finally, just before the evening service, we were able to contact him. He was planning on coming to the service anyway and would take them all home with him and his wife. They were both very wonderful Christians. Before the service, he had made other phone contacts with other sheriffs in nearby towns and had them doing some investigating. It was not long till a back up soon arrived.

It was my turn to conduct the service that Sunday evening. Because it was so hot, the side door of the church was left open. During the service, I noticed that the family, who was sitting with Jean, seemed a little restless. The sheriff and his wife were sitting right behind them. What I did not know, was that the angry daddy was standing at the side door with a gun. Soon a sheriff's car came around the corner and the man with the gun ran, throwing the gun into a vacant lot across the street. The family was quite relieved to see him go.

After the service, the family went home with the sheriff and was protected there that night. We closed the church and walked to the parsonage, which was located in back of the church. We had no sooner unlocked the door and gone in, locking the door behind us, when there was a loud knocking on the door. Since the door had a window in it, and since the porch light was still on, we could see who was doing the pounding. You guessed it, there was the very angry and drunk daddy, yelling threats at us. We tried to talk to him, but were not making any progress. Still upset, he finally left, and we were glad.

The next two days were spent finding out the best legal advice for this young mother and her children. They were to leave the area that night right away, without any further contact with him, so they could start a new life.

The mother, Jean, and I had gone to the district attorney's office, which was about thirty miles away, to get final instructions for the mother. Looking out of the office window, we saw the daddy parked across the street. How were we to get back home without his seeing us? We prayed! When it was time to leave, a big semi truck parked in front of the office, thus enabling us to leave without being seen by him and to get home safely!

On Wednesday nights, we always had Bible study for the adults and a special class for the children. A final call had to be made concerning the family, so Jean went out of town to do it, since there were no private phone lines at that time. I started our Bible studies with the two groups together. Jean was a little late getting back from making the phone call and had just received word from the tavern owner that this man was there, making claims that he was going to the church and kill all the Christians and the missionaries. Since he had a gun, we had better all go home until the sheriff could get him and take the gun away. So Bible study was cancelled and we stayed with a family that lived a few miles away.

Finally, the gun was confiscated and he was told to stay away from us and all the Christians. Several people had been deputized and ordered to shoot him if he tried anything. The investigations had proved that he had a bad record and could not be trusted. A few days later, he walked by the parsonage and yelled at us, but he kept walking as we ignored him. Finally he left the community when he could not find his wife. The last news we heard about him was that he was incarcerated for life in another state.

His wife and children started a new life far from him and continued to grow in the Lord. The son was killed by a hit and run driver, when he was in high school. He left a good solid testimony. The mother continued to be very active in Christian work and shared her testimony often, until she went home to be with the Lord.

Yes, God's protecting hand was upon me, while He was making my feet like hinds' feet upon the high places of trial.

CHAPTER 6

Therapy Intensified

How easy it is to fall into a schedule and become comfortable in it. The time comes, however, when the Master Physician sees the need for a change in therapy. At this time a better opportunity to fully develop feet, like hinds' feet, is given.

In 1957, our National Director asked if I would be willing to train a new girl. We would have to go to a new little

The Grange Hall

community to start and develop a work for the Lord. With fear and trembling, I said, "Yes," and entered a new high, treacherous place of responsibility. When Louise James and I arrived in this rural area, we discovered there was no church. All public meetings were held in the grange hall. Each Sunday morning, we had to go early, clean, and arrange chairs and such for the church service. If anyone came to help us, we were very thankful.

Housing was hard to find, so we lived in a motel room. Fixing meals was difficult, but we were invited out for many of our meals. Later, a travel trailer was provided for us to live in and that was much nicer, even though it was small. We had a beautiful view of the ocean. While we lived in this little trailer, we experienced one of those wind storms, for which the Oregon coast is famous. As the trailer rocked back and forth, we found out what it must be like to be caught out at sea in a small boat when a storm arises. The wind took down the power pole between our trailer and the one next to us and fell on it, instead of ours. We were thankful that the trailer was empty and no one was hurt. Not a single wire touched ours. Truly we were divinely protected!

This was a time when many high places would be experienced. Louise had to leave the work, because of her mother's illness and she was desperately needed at home. When she left, I was without transportation, leaving me in a very difficult high place. When we gathered for our midweek Bible study and prayer meeting, I asked the people to pray about this need. It was unforgettable to hear the little seven year old girl say, "I'll take that request." Oh, the power of such a child-like prayer! All she said was, "Lord, Zelma needs a car and partner to get your work done." She finished with a hearty "amen." A partner did arrive—on a bus.

She did not even know how to drive. Well, little Linda was anxious at our next prayer time to pray again. She thanked the Lord for my new partner and just reminded the Lord that we sure needed a car to do His work. Another hearty "amen." God honored that little girl's persistence and faith. Money came in for the car and a very nice used car became available. A mechanic took us eighty miles to look at it and to check it out, to make sure it was worth having. That day, we drove home rejoicing all the way. God had sent in enough money for the down payment. A little church in another state decided to send money each month for car expenses, so that helped with the monthly payments.

Our little prayer partner was so eager to pray at our next meeting. This time she said, "Dear Lord, thank you so much for a car for the missionaries. I know you will pay for it, too. Amen." Some important lessons were being taught to us by a little seven year old.

Before the first payment was due, God had brought in enough money to pay off the car!

The check came all the way from Japan. A military couple, who were stationed there, heard about my need from a friend. They had some tithe money they had been praying about and God directed them to my car need. They did not know me, but they felt that this was God's will. Not only was my faith strengthened, but I was reminded that "God works in mysterious ways, His wonders to perform." Distance means nothing to Him. Something else was brought to my attention. God allows me to walk in high places, not only to strengthen me in faith, and witness His power, but that those around me may be encouraged and strengthened. Each high place of trouble, suffering or responsibility that my Master foot physician allows me to face is always witnessed by many other people. The way I walk on these high places will somehow affect those who watch. In 1958, a village missionary arrived to continue the work there, and soon a new high place of responsibility would be mine. I would be following in my grandfather's footsteps. He had been a circuit-riding preacher, starting many little churches in the southern part of the country.

Rev. W. H. Hodges, Zelma's circuit-riding grandfather

We were asked to go to another community in Oregon. This time we found a small Sunday school going that met in a school house. They even had a nice little house with all the furniture we would need. The people were very gracious and greeted us with open arms. A food shower was given, ten gallons of gas for our car, and even a supply of firewood—all stacked and ready to use!

It did not take long to get church services started, as well as Bible studies, youth programs, and children's classes. It was exciting to work with these people and see the church grow. A community just a few miles away over the mountain heard about the work there and asked if we would open their closed church and get things going. All the missionary arrangements were made and the circuit riding began. We went to one little community early for a worship service and arrived back at the first community for their worship service. They conducted their own Sunday School.

This little church had been closed long enough for rats and mice to take over. A good long work day soon had that place clean and shining for services. How hard the people worked to get this accomplished and the excitement of having their first church service in years was contagious. The missionaries did extensive visitation, notices were put up, and announcements were made on the radio.

I will never forget an eighty year old man who came out for the first service. He had not been to church for twenty years. His son, who lived in another town, heard the radio announcement about the opening of this church for services, so he called his dad long distance to tell him about it. He was so grateful to be able to come and attend services.

The old pump organ gave a quaint atmosphere to the church. My co-worker was able to play it, so that helped out with the singing—so we thought! It did not take long for us to realize that when she hit the high C note, it would sound off for the rest of the service, loud and clear! Trying to give a message with a high C note sounding off was an unusual experience, to say the least! We finally gave up using the organ. God had pity on us and a piano was given to the church.

How often the tears would come as I thanked the Lord for the privilege of opening a closed church. To be able to ring the church bell and see souls come to know Christ in a personal way was joy unspeakable!

About twenty miles west, another community was calling for help. As we looked at our schedule, we decided we could work them in on Sunday afternoons. This proved to be a very exciting work because we saw results immediately. At the first service, three people came to know Jesus. The second service, twelve more souls received Christ as their personal Savior. What an exhilarating day that was!

I was certainly treading upon a very high place of responsibility, when my partner had to quit the work, leaving me with the following schedule:

Sundays 8:45 AM Sunday school at 2nd church
9:45 AM Worship at 2nd church
11:00 AM Worship at 1st church
2:00 P.M. Sunday school at 3rd church
3:00 P.M. Worship service at 3rd church
7:30P.M. Evening service at 1st church
Tuesdays 7:30 P.M. Bible study for all three churches at 1st church
Wednesdays 3:30 P.M. Childrens' class at 1st church
Thursdays 3:30 P.M. Childrens' class at 3rd church

Often, grandfather Hodges came to mind. He had traveled by horseback or bicycle to his churches. At least, I had a Volkswagen.

Help soon arrived. Annette Jones was sent to join me in this massive endeavor. She was a very talented person, with her own car—filling a very definite need! She took over the third little church, while I continued on with the other two. This proved to be a real blessing and help! In 1959, two village mission couples were sent to continue the ministry in these communities.

Zelma's little bug

Annette and Zelma

Annette and I headed for a small community in northern California. We started a Sunday school and church services in the grange hall, the local meeting place. This required early Sunday morning janitorial work for us, as the grange hall was used for many Saturday night activities. Sometimes it was a real mess and not very conducive to a worship service. It was cold enough that we needed to build a fire in the two huge oil drums that had been made into wood burning stoves. It was such a big building that it seemed to take forever to get it warm enough. After much visitation and hard work, the response was delightful. The people kept bringing new friends and the attendance continued to grow. Annette had to take a medical leave. I continued the work until all the trees in the area caused my asthma to flare up. I, too, had to take a leave. Another team of rural missionaries was sent to replace us. God blessed mightily and used these ladies. Eventually the work grew and a church was built to the glory of God!

I came home to rest and recupe a bit. As soon as I began to feel better, I was asked to check around southern California to see if there might be any needs for Christian leadership in the rural areas. I began to pray with an open map before me and my attention was captured by a small town in the high desert. The urge to check this place was unusual. Wanting someone to accompany me on this jaunt, I asked my sister to go and she agreed.

The next morning we were up early and on our way. We drove around looking for a church building and we found a house with a sign in front which read, "Community Bible Church."

We went next door to ask about it, but they did not seem to know much. We asked if people gathered there on Sundays for services. "I don't know," was blurted out. When we realized we were getting nowhere with them, we went

to the post office for information. They did not know either, but gave us a name of a man to ask. That lead turned up a very congenial couple, who were even anxious to talk with us! As I shared about the work of Village Missions and gave them some literature, tears welled up in their eyes. They began by telling us that they had just been praying about what should be done regarding the situation. The retired minister, who had been driving eighty miles one way each Sunday to hold services, had just told them the past Sunday that he could no longer come because of his health. Arrangements were made for me to come back the next Sunday to have a meeting and present the work of Village Missions to that small congregation. They asked me to stay for an evening service, so I did. A short business meeting was called to vote on whether or not to have a village missionary.

Thinking my part was over, I left for home. I had made a survey of the area and sent all reports to headquarters. A few days later, I received word from Mr. Duff, our national director, that the little church had voted for a missionary, and had requested to have me come! What a shock that was!

At this time there was no couple available to place there, so I was to go and serve as soon as the house was ready for me. Just before I had arrived to present Village Missions, the house had been donated to the church, in hopes they would have a full time pastor someday. The Lord had worked this all out and I was humbled and challenged as I stepped onto another high place of responsibility!

The parsonage

In May, 1960, the little house was to be occupied. It was even furnished, so the moving process was simple—just unload my car. I received word that Annette was ready to come and join me again. That was refreshing news! We learned that the old house we were meeting in was a historical building. It had been the over night stopping place for the twenty mule team borox wagon when it came through. There was an old barn behind it where they kept the mules. Things had changed since the railroad had come. The house had been altered to make one big room across the front, which was used for worship service. The little rooms in the back were used for Sunday school classes. As the congregation grew, the old barn was cleaned out and used for our teenagers.

The parsonage was located on the famous Route 66. Next door was what one called "downtown," consisting of a motel, restaurant, and service station. Across the highway, and running parallel with it, were railroad tracks and another little road. The church was on this road. It took some adjusting to get accustomed to the eighty daily trains that came barreling through.

The extreme heat (115-120 degrees) was another adjustment we had to make. Once again, the Lord God was our strength and help.

We always tried to have fun activities for our youth groups, no matter where we might be. It seemed just right to have a hobo convention in that old barn. Everyone would dress in their best hobo attire, because there would be a crowning of the king and queen of the convention. Thirty-eight teens came out for the big event. Did we ever have some unique hoboes! It was a tricky job for the judges to choose the king and queen. Much to our surprise and shock, a real hobo came. He had seen the posters we had put up advertising the convention and thought it was for real hoboes. When he found out that it was a church group, he was quick to be on his way; but not before receiving an invitation to stay for a handout, along with some Christian literature. We learned later that there was a real hobo camp not far away from us.

The old barn where we had Sunday school and youth activities, including our hobo convention

There was much physical work to do, along with all the spiritual challenges. Getting that old barn in shape was a real chore. Cleaning and putting in some kind of air conditioning was a must to make it bearable and useable at all. It was not very glamorous or inviting, but that did not hinder the work from growing. We saw a steady growth in all services. The need for a church building became quite obvious when we tried to squeeze one hundred people into the building for Sunday school and church. We felt we had been put in with a shoe horn, but we did manage to get everybody inside. The trustees began to look for suitable lots to build a church—this time away from the railroad tracks. It was extremely difficult to give a message when trains interrupted. All that could be done was to stop and wait for the train to pass through and then start again, until the next one roared by. Lots were found and a down payment was made. My oldest brother, Bill, who was an architect in the Riverside area, was willing to come out and help by drawing up plans and making blueprints.

Our youth group wanted to help, too. At Christmas, they put on a live manger scene. It was a big project, but their enthusiasm became very contagious, and soon many people in the community were involved. The men helped in the building part, even a little church bank was built for donations. The ladies worked on the costumes making them look very authentic. The young people worked on the many other details, such as securing live animals. Calico ghost town, about seven miles away, had two donkeys which they were willing to let us use. They were real pets and used to crowds of people being around. Their names were Christmas and Carol. Two of the girls went up to Calico to get them and ride them back. What a time they had! Christmas became very stubborn. They tried to lead her, pull her, and even push her. She would not budge. Finally, one of the girls got on her and began to sing, "Onward Christian Soldiers," and Christmas took off, with Carol right behind her. The girls kept singing all the way home. A white goat, named "Tinker Bell," added much to the manger scene, along with some chickens roosting on the fence.

The young people came out each night to take their turn on one of the two shifts—an hour each of acting the part of Mary, Joseph and the shepherds. A doll was used for Baby Jesus. Others took turns at the registration table, where the guests were invited to sign the guest book and receive a beautiful tract, telling the true meaning of Christmas. The little church bank was on the table so donations could be made, if people desired.

The high spirits of the young people had been dampened on the opening night, as one of their classmates had been killed in an auto accident. When the crowds began to gather and the newspaper cameras began to flash, their spirits began to soar again.

Soon the big announcement was made. The live manger scene had won in the contest of all the Christmas decorations in the desert! The first prize was thirty-five dollars, for the church building fund.

The publicity that followed was fantastic as the local radio station and newspaper kept the live nativity scene very much alive and in the limelight all week. Each evening brought new excitement and anticipation as the crowds gathered. The big, blazing, gas torches which were placed in front of the scene drew some. Others were attracted by the big star above the scene, which had its own spot light. The sweet Christmas music that filled the air caused others to stop. As the revolving spotlight flashed different colors across the live animals and figures, the onlookers stood in deep thought. Once in awhile, Tinker Bell would take a devoted look at the Baby in the manger. At other times there was laughter as Christmas and Carol would put on an act of their own. What pets they were and how much they were enjoying all the attention they were receiving!

The big excitement came one night when, after closing the scene, the young people gathered in the parsonage to open the little church bank and found three fifty dollar bills, along with other bills! Some had never seen a fifty dollar bill before. The money that had come in was a real inspiration for the youth, but the new faces in the church brought an even greater thrill. On Christmas Eve, the last night of the scene, the public was invited to join the youth group to gather around the nativity scene and sing favorite Christmas carols. Many people gathered for this event and it proved to be a special blessing to every one.

The prize winning nativity scene

One of the greatest delights of the whole week was when one of the travelers, just passing through, stopped to see what the big crowds were all about. He was so deeply moved that he could not continue his journey; he went next door and got a motel room for the night. Before going to bed, he read the little Christmas tract he had received. God spoke to his heart and he placed his faith in the Lord Jesus. The next day, he told one of the townspeople that he had been an atheist until he stopped at the nativity scene. This was the first time he had realized what Christmas was all about. How thankful he was for a group of young people who had made Christmas real to him.

Each day seemed to bring new experiences and adjustments in my life, as I was walking on high places of trials and responsibilities. Learning to live with the extreme heat, wind, and sand was constantly before us. Our days were crammed full. One day we were asked to conduct a graveside service for a little baby of one of our families. Since we had not been out to the cemetery yet, we decided to drive out and check it before the service. The road was sand and more sand and nothing but barren desert—no trees, flowers, or grass. This tiny place truly represented death. Tumbleweeds were plentiful and here and there was a sprout of sage brush or greasewood. Even the rattlesnakes stayed hidden during the day in order to try to escape the intense heat. They, too, represented death. The graves were marked with primitive wooden crosses and piles of rocks. Some had fences built around them to keep the coyotes out. What a desolate place!

The service was to be held at 1:30. We met the undertaker, who drove us out to the cemetery. It was one hundred and twenty degrees that day and he told us we should stay in the car until the time for the service. He left the engine running so we could have air-conditioning. When we stepped out by that little grave, it did not take long for the soles of my feet to begin burning. My shoes had thin soles and the sand was so hot that I had blisters on my feet by the time it was over.

Following that, we had two childrens' classes. As the Bible story was given, a little girl wanted to ask Jesus into her heart and life. We were all thrilled at her understanding of God's Word, as well as her prayer of commitment after the class. It was all I could do to keep the tears back, as I had just witnessed a new birth in Christ—especially after just burying this little girl's sister. Death and a new birth, all in the same day, and in the same family!

The time came when we felt the need for the parsonage to have a real yard—something other than sand, dirt, and tumbleweeds. Picking up the trash that the wind had blown in, or that the hitch-hikers had left behind, turned out to be an endless task. Everyone agreed that we needed a front and backyard, all fenced in with grass and shrubs. An eager crew volunteered to help. We were reminded that a load of fertilizer would be needed to get anything to grow. One of the men said he would order it as his donation to the work. Others helped putting up the fence, while others started digging and preparing the ground for planting grass.

Later one evening, Annette went out back to do something and discovered a large pile of fertilizer dumped near our back gate. She came in all excited, declaring, "The fertilizer is here!" Right away we started calling the men to come and help us. As they well knew, and we had discovered, nothing is ever left outside the fence over night in this community, or it would be gone in the morning. The crew arrived and worked very hard to get all that fertilizer inside our fence and spread all over the front and back yards. They worked so late that we had to turn on the yard lights. The next morning, we saw the man who was to order the fertilizer, to thank him. It was quite a shock, to say the least, when he informed us that he had not ordered it yet! About that same time, the owner of the motel, restaurant and gas station next door to the parsonage, discovered that their fertilizer which had been delivered in the back, close to our back gate, had disappeared and was scattered neatly over the parsonage yard. They could hardly believe their eyes!

The next big step was for Annette and me to muster up enough courage to go to our neighbors and make things right. The reason it was so difficult was that we had been visiting them trying to gain their confidence, in hopes they would soon become part of our church family. We went over to the restaurant, ordered a cup of coffee, and asked if the owners were there. We found them in one of the back rooms, doing some paper work. They invited us in and were very pleasant to us, so it was easy to apologize to them. When we offered to pay for it, the money was refused with the explanation, "We have never laughed so hard in all our lives. This has done us more good than money or fertilizer. Just to think it was the missionaries who took it this time!" Believe it or not, this was the beginning of a real friendship and these dear people finally became very active in our church. God takes what we do, mistakes and all, and works them together for good and His glory, too! The parsonage became one of the most popular stops in the community with people coming and going frequently.

Yes, this project was worth the time and effort, even if the fertilizer was "stolen." We, as missionaries, however, do not recommend this as a correct or ideal way to get new church members.

The replacement for the first Community Bible Church

CHAPTER 7

Therapy Extended

In 1962, a village missionary was sent to the high desert to continue that work and I was to enter a new phase in my endeavors. I was asked to be a field representative, which simply meant that I would become a "portable" missionary—full time travel, going and preparing each new community for the placement of a village missionary couple. Often finding and preparing adequate housing for the arriving couples was a time consuming experience. Some times I would be a "fill-in" between missionaries when moves were being made. I also would be going to Bible schools and colleges to present our work to the students. I was headed for some new experiences which would take daily exercise for my spiritual progress upon some very high places of trouble, suffering, and responsibility!!

Once again, I found myself working alone, as Annette's physical problems made it necessary for her to leave the work. She was missed by everyone!

My missionary journey then took me to Colorado. I started out in a beautiful and quaint little community. The Wayside Chapel was picturesque with the colorful Rocky peaks for the background.

The colors were absolutely gorgeous! Cattle ranches penetrated the valley with high mesas surrounding them. In the summer time the mesas were used for their cow camps. Up on one of the mesas was a small school house and a few families who lived there year round. One night a

The Wayside Chapel

week I would go up to that school house and have Sunday school for them. Sometimes the road would wash out, so I could not go every week. The people were very gracious and pleased when I did make it. My Sundays were filled with the services at the Wayside Chapel.

While filling in between missionaries, I was asked to speak at the baccalaureate service, as well as to have a part in their graduation. They had a large class of seven seniors that year. That was a rare experience!

After a few months there, the next assignment was in a small logging community in Idaho with a forestry station, which helped to keep the population occupied. There was a church with some mature Christians. What a blessing to work with these dear people! At that time there was no Sunday school class for the teenagers. I had attended their football games and enjoyed these young people so much and I felt they needed a class, too. Step one was to get a list of all their names. Step two was to pray for each of them by name. Step three was to send out invitations and talk to as many as possible about having a class for them.

The Saturday night before the class was to start, I was so excited, and yet burdened, for these kids that I decided to pray for each one of them again. In the middle of my prayer time, the phone rang and a very anxious voice told me that there had been a serious car accident and some of our teenagers were involved. Arriving at the scene of the accident, I saw that the car had gone off the road and over an embankment. Bodies were scattered all over the hillside—some for whom I had just been praying. I was overwhelmed with the thought, "Are they dead or alive?" By that time, the whole community had arrived and was making stretchers out of removed doors and transporting them to the nurse's house. The long distance the ambulances had to come, along with the ice and snow, made it quite a chore for them to get there. The nurse had begun to treat the victims as best she could until the doctor arrived. Two young people were wounded seriously enough to be hospitalized, but were home again in a few days. I continued my prayer time that night, but with the young people and their parents! We did get that Sunday school class started and God did bless abundantly!

While filling in there, I received word that another little community several miles away was eager to have its own village missionary. So part of my time there was spent surveying the possibilities of having services in some other communities.

December arrived with all of its Christmas activities. A Sunday school program and a cantata were in the making. Word came that the new missionary would be arriving, too. This was a very busy time for all of us. I had been asked to sing a solo part in the cantata. I had promised one of the communities that had been checked that I would come for Christmas and hold a service for them, too.

In between all of this activity, I was not feeling very well, so decided to work in a visit to the doctor. He took a blood test, checking for diabetes, with results in a week. When he learned of my schedule, he warned me to leave right after the Christmas service. Since that area gets so much snow, it was easily possible to be snowed in for the winter. Then if there were diabetes, treatment would not be available. Because many people were praying, God held back the snow enabling me to meet with these dear people for the Christmas service. What a delightful time we had! It was an unforgettable Christmas! I was able to get back down the mountain to the doctor before the snow hit.

What a surprise and blessing to find one of the couples from the community I had just been serving, at the doctor's office waiting for me! They did not want me to be alone when the test results were given. It was wonderful to have their support when I did find that it was diabetes. They took me out to lunch to help me get started on the new diet. It was necessary to stay close to the doctor, so they invited me to stay with them, while adjusting to the insulin and learning to care for myself. I was treading upon another high place, this time of suffering and responsibility. *"And we know that all things work together for good to them that love God, to them who are the called according to His purpose."* Romans 8:28 KJV God in His great wisdom knew that there would be encounters with many diabetics along my path, who could use some words of encouragement. I needed to experience this high place, and make spiritual progress, in order to help others.

As I continued my travels, there was a short stay in Colorado high up in the ski country. Such a beautiful community it was! There was a new town and a new church. The old town had been located down in the valley, which was flooded to make a beautiful lake. Because the old church was a historical landmark, it was moved up next to the new church and parsonage. Many visitors came to see and learn about the history of the town, which became a resort area. We had missionaries there, even before the town was moved. It is always a thrill to visit these communities and learn their history. But it was better yet to see the enormous results our missionaries have experienced.

California had a need in a little place called Sierraville in the High Sierras, so I was soon on my way. I went as far as Reno, Nevada, and was told the roads were closed because of flooding, melting snow, and rock slides. It was necessary to be there the next day for services. It was time to have the car serviced so decided to have that done and prayed while waiting. When the car was finished, I asked the police about road conditions. They told me the roads had just been opened only as far as Sierraville. That was good enough for me! God is never late! Once again, He was making my feet like hinds' feet.

Being on the road again and traveling in different states, thirty-six field contacts were made before ending up in New Mexico to be a fill-in one more time. There were some interruptions. For example, I would like to call January, 1964, "My Journeys."

The journey was long and the weather was bad.
But He gave a song that made me glad.
Many stops were made along the way,
With missionaries and friends who had much to say.
The times of prayer and thanksgiving, too,

Made each step a blessing and my strength renewed.
Many steps were taken in a different way,
That His purpose be filled from day to day.
The week at a missionary conference was such a thrill
That none who attended could escape seeking His will.
The journey back was just as long,
But in the heart was still that song.
The steps and stops were altered a bit
To do some field work that was very fit.
The last stretch of the journey, my faith was tested,
But God in His faithfulness, His promises true,
Brought me back safely, His work to do.

> *"And, behold, I am with thee, and will keep thee in all places to which thou goest, and will bring thee again into this land; for I will not leave thee, until I have done that which I have spoken to thee of." Genesis 28:15 kjv*

> *"Commit thy way unto the Lord; trust also in him, and he shall bring it to pass." Psalm 32:5 KJV*

What a blessing these verses proved to be as this journey was completed. It was awesome to be back in New Mexico to continue the work there until a missionary could come to take over the work.

From 1964 to 1976, the field work continued—driving many miles, working in nineteen states, surveying fields, and contacting Bible schools in Canada and the United States for prospective missionaries. As I journeyed upon many high places, He was always there to see me through, and all the time, making my feet like hinds' feet. *"Faithful is He who is calling you [to Himself] and utterly trustworthy and He will also do it [that is, fulfill His call by hallowing and keeping you]."* I Thessalonians 5:24 AMP How true this verse has been proven in my life.

Being a "portable" missionary allowed me to carry only the bare necessities. The good old standbys were a toaster oven, coffee pot, a very small set of unbreakable dishes, silverware, and one saucepan, along with linens and bedding. For the cold country, an electric blanket helped. You see, traveling in a Volkswagen, one travels very lightly. Other necessities included my office supplies, typewriter and a few books. Entering a new community each time brought questions about what kind of housing would be available. Sometimes I would stay with a family. Other times there was a house with a bed, table, and chair—not mentioning their conditions! Camping at its best!!

A great variety of buildings had been made into parsonages; for example, a motel where each room had an outside door. Another time it was a schoolhouse with a full basement made into bedrooms, giving multiple choices for sleeping quarters. The upstairs was divided into a kitchen/dining area and a huge living room—wonderful for Bible studies. Oh, yes, there was a "his" and "her" bathroom! The most unique parsonage was a former hospital. A big corporation owned the whole town, but as plans for relocation progressed, the hospital was closed first. Consent was given for it to be used as missionary quarters. I called the room chosen for my bedroom the "recovery room," not realizing it had actually been the hospital's recovery room. Several nice little apartments, travel trailers, and mobile homes, also, were home for me. Wherever I hung my hat was home. The people always did their best to make me feel comfortable.

CHAPTER 8

Double-Barreled Missionaries in High Places

In 1976, my traveling days were beginning to affect my health, so Betty Edwards was sent to help me out. What a blessing! Now traveling would be much easier as Betty could help drive. She also had a nice travel trailer, so we didn't have to pack and unpack at each stop. We always had our house with us. After working in several places in California and Oregon getting communities ready for a village missionary, we were assigned to go to a beautiful, rural area on

Zelma and Betty–the double-barreled missionaries, what we were called at one place where we worked.

the southern Oregon coast. I had started the work there twenty years previously. This small church had many ups and downs because of the ever-changing population. Being a logging area, work depended upon whether or not the local mills were operating. Village missionaries had worked there through the years, but it was very difficult because of the changes. It was a rough place of responsibility.

The church was dilapidated, floors were rotting, weeds and briars were taking over, and the few people who were attending had lost hope. The name of this place was "Ophir," and our favorite phrase was, "Ophir goodness' sake!"

The last thing we wanted to see was the church doors closed. God worked in our hearts and extended His love and strength so we could *"walk, and not stand still in terror."*

The first weeks were spent praying, as we visited each home leaving a beautiful Stonecroft Life Publication booklet, which gives the way to find God and His free gift of salvation. Soon we began to see results. People began coming to Sunday school and church. Children's classes were started after school and a youth group was formed. Folks began to see the need for repairing and remodeling the church building.

A new peaked roof with a steeple replaced the flat, leaky one. Cement floors replaced the rotting wood ones. The youth group did baby sitting, had car washes and bake sales, and did all sorts of odd jobs, in order to have a new carpet installed. A brand new mobile home was placed right near the church, which made a neat place for the missionaries to live. The muddy parking lot was covered with gravel and the whole grounds were landscaped beautifully, after many work days. We had a lovely little white church on a hill overlooking the ocean, with highway 101 running along the foot of the hill. From the highway, a twenty-five foot cross, outlined with white rocks filled with blood red ice plant could be seen on the hillside. This was quite an attraction as tour buses would stop so people could take pictures. Our deepest desire for this place was beginning to come true. People were turning to God and the whole community expressed their appreciation for the church. Hearing the church bell ringing every Sunday was a constant reminder of God and His love for them.

One day when we were out visiting, we met an elderly couple who made it clear to us they were not church people, nor did they even want the subject brought up. They said it

The first church building at Ophir

was OK to visit them, if we did not bring up religion. Their unscriptural language showed there was no Christian background. Hard as it was to not talk about the Lord to them, we continued to visit them, but honored their request not to talk about God. We just loved them in the Lord. Since they had no family, we checked in on them often. We "adopted"

Remodeling the Ophir church

The finished product

View of the church from highway 101

them and had invited them to our home for Christmas Eve dinner. Eventually they showed up in church and began to attend regularly. One Sunday, the wife accepted Christ as her Savior. The change in her language and her life was magnificent. She became anxious for her husband to become a Christian.

It was Christmas Eve and we were invited to their house for dinner. We had prayed that he would bring up the subject of salvation that night, if the time was right for him to accept the Lord as his Savior. The evening wore on and we wondered if he would ever ask or say anything to open the way to talk to him about God. As time for us to leave approached, he suddenly asked, "How do you join that church?" We explained the way of salvation—it was not joining the church, but having a personal relationship with Jesus Christ by inviting Him into his heart and life. He replied, "Yes, I believe I can do that." Then we had a precious time of prayer with them thanking the Lord for their salvation. What a marvelous Christmas gift!

One day the wife became seriously ill and in a short time, she went to be with the Lord. It was a dreadfully hard time for the husband, so we helped him with all the necessary arrangements. We felt real peace and joy, just knowing she was with her Savior.

We continued to daily check in on Fred and do all we could to help him. He had some wonderful Christian neighbors who were good to help him, also. One day he called us to tell us he was going to California to visit his sister. Sometime later, we received a call from an attorney to let us know the church had received a bequest from one of our members. Unbeknown to us, Fred had gone to heaven and had left their entire estate to the church!! We were overwhelmed to say the least! Our biggest desire for the church was for it

Helen and Fred Taylor, the church's benefactors

to become self supporting before we left and had to turn it over to another village missionary. When the estate was all settled, this desire was fulfilled.

About that time, my physical condition was deteriorating and I was asking God what I should do. I was not up to a new assignment or much travel. As we prayed about it, I felt the need for some time off and Betty felt the Lord was leading her back into teaching. Since we were able to work so well together, we decided to stay together. I could rest and she could teach school again. Mr. Duff, the Village Mission director, had a married couple to come and replace us. I took a medical leave and we moved to northern California, where Betty began teaching in a Christian school. This time period was not easy for me, as my spirit wanted to get busy for the Lord, but the old flesh was experiencing burnout, another high place of suffering. The question came, "How long would I be climbing this high place"? Isaiah 40:31 KJV flooded my soul. *"They that wait upon the Lord shall renew their strength; they shall mount up with wings like eagles; they shall run, and not be weary; and they shall walk, and not faint."* No, I did not need to stand still in terror, but to walk. God did not intend for me to run upon the high places, but to walk. When we are rushing, it is easy to run ahead of God. He wants us to wait upon Him. That is the only way to renew our strength. When I began to wait and relax in His strength and power, things began to change.

The need for some Bible studies was an open door in the mobile home park where we lived. As the Lord blessed these, He gave me a vision and a burden for Bible studies in all of northern California.

One day as I was praying, I asked God to show me if He wanted me to go back full time with Stonecroft Ministries, this time working with the Friendship Bible Coffee program. The fleece was put out, asking that headquarters would call me (with absolutely no contact from me) and ask me to do this. It took less than a week to receive that call! When they asked if I felt like doing some Bible studies, I told them it was already being done, and it was thrilling! What a marvelous outreach and ministry! Now I would be working in the cities and the villages! A big high place of responsibility!

Out came the California map. Much prayer for guidance was needed as I perused the map. God provided me with a car, once again, and off I went to make those many contacts. It was not long till people were requesting help in their towns to get Bible studies started. After a number of introductory meetings, training workshops, finding guide and coordinators in different areas, numerous Bible studies were sprouting up and growing. Prayers and countless miles of travel were paying off. How precious to walk in high places, when God is in charge. My strength had been renewed!

Six years later, Betty had a strong desire to go back to teaching in the public schools. She felt her ministry would be enlarged. The idea that "light shines better in a dark place than a lighted one" kept ringing in her heart. The Christian school was a well-lit place. We began to pray for guidance. The Bible studies were going well and there were some wonderful coordinators to keep them going. We also knew that wherever we went, there would be a need for home Bible studies.

The Lord gave us both a vision for Moreno Valley in southern California, although we knew no one there. Its population was exploding, creating a vast need for teachers. It was a giant step of faith, but we moved down south, believing God to give Betty a job where He wanted her to teach. She took a job at a local produce stand for the summer while waiting to hear from one of the number of schools to which she had applied. It was not till August that one she had not even applied to, called her to her first love—first grade—in a brand new school! Once again, God had honored that step of faith! We did not have much money, but were so excited that we felt it was time for a celebration. It so happened that a fast food place had a sale, so we made merry with a ten cent burrito! There was no one ever happier! Needless to say, the doors opened wide for Bible studies and one was started right away.

God provided a nice, large rental house close to Betty's school, so we could have lots of meetings. The need for a Christian Women's Club was heavy on our hearts. Stonecroft was contacted about the need. We moved into the house on Saturday and on Monday, two National Representatives arrived to start the club! By the time they appeared, I had compiled quite a list of names of woman interested in having a Christian Women's Club. Before long, there was a club, as well as Friendship Bible Coffees, with guides and coordinators to help.

Betty made numerous contacts with her school parents and guided Bible studies with some of the mothers of her first graders. Several of them came to Christian Women's Club, along with a number of school personnel. Her ministry was rather exciting! The Bible studies continue to grow in this area. A neat consulting coordinator helps to keep things moving.

There was another unique ministry for us in this place. We started a "B" (Bible) club in our home, where the neighborhood children came once a week after school to sing, learn Bible verses, and listen to Bible stories. Over the years, dozens of children came to know the Lord Jesus as their own Savior. Parents often were in attendance, also. Truly, God has blessed us with an awesome ministry!

In spite of all the blessings around me, I found myself walking upon the high place of health problems. My doctor kept asking when I was going to retire, so I began to pray about it. The Lord reminded me that He had blessed with wonderful people to carry on the work of Friendship Bible Coffees and the Christian Women's Club. Since I was getting "less young," I felt it was time to retire. The Lord also reminded me that I was not retiring from Him, only the work that I had been doing for forty years.

Little did I know what a difficult high place was approaching. God had allowed me to serve Him all these years in a public way and now a new life style would begin. Feelings of loneliness, detachment, and isolation were overwhelming. But once again, God reminded me that a prayer ministry is like that. He even went apart to pray. It was lonely when the disciples fell asleep while He was praying in Gethsemane. It was lonely when He hung on the cross and prayed. Jesus reminded me that I am never alone for He said, "*Lo, I am with you always.*" Matthew 28:20 KJV The ministry of prayer is becoming progressively exciting and rewarding as I see Him working in incredible ways. There will always be high places and hard lessons to learn, but He is my strength. I have a wonderful, powerful God!

CHAPTER 9

Lessons to be Learned While Walking in High Places

Life in itself is a learning process. We are not conscious of this until we start walking upon the high difficult places, then we become aware of the lessons God is trying to teach us. Sometimes our attention span is short, so God has to work with us over and over again till we learn the important lesson that He wants us to comprehend.

One of these lessons is faith. Oh, yes, I had placed my faith in the Lord Jesus when I was a child, but it took some doing to get me to the place of trusting Him with everything. Have you ever had a month that was longer than your paycheck? Surely I am not alone on this. What a dilemma!

One time, on a new field, the money was gone and food supply was scarce. We had two eggs, two potatoes, and two onions—that was it! The car's gas gauge was on empty and it was another whole week before payday. Sunday arrived and we walked to church. After the service, a teenage girl asked to come home with us, so she could come to the evening service. It was time for another step of faith. We didn't have much to serve for dinner and had no gas to take her home after church. She had walked eight miles to get to church that morning. We opened our home and shared what we had. I fried the potatoes and scrambled the eggs in them. It looked like the next menu would be onion soup. We gathered around the table and gave thanks for the food and for our friend with whom we could share it. We also gave thanks for the gas He would provide for the car. Just about that time, there was a knock at the door. It was a lady we did not know because she was from out of state and was there on a fishing trip. She explained how excited she was that we were there to get a church started—an answer to her prayers. They came there every year to go fishing, but hated to miss church. She was even more thrilled when she discovered we were with the Stonecroft Ministries. As she left, she handed me a ten dollar bill, saying, "Maybe this will help buy gas for your car or whatever you need for the work here." As we sat down to continue our meal, we felt the need to thank the Lord for the gas money. Now we could take our guest home that evening. Before we finished dinner, another knock came on the door. This time it was a lady from the church. She told how she had just been to the grocery store and felt she should get us some food, so presented us with a big bag of groceries—enough to last for that week! God taught us a lot about faith that day! Our friend was deeply moved also.

As I started to share these lessons, I realized that Galatians 5:22, 23 KJV was really what was taking place in my life. It says, "*But the fruit of the Spirit is love, joy, peace, long suffering, gentleness, goodness, faith, meekness, self-control; against such there is no law.*" All of these things were needed in my life, when walking upon the high places. God in His love and mercy was teaching me.

A hard lesson to be learned was walking at God's pace. By nature I am an anxious human being and very impatient. It was necessary to learn that God's clock keeps perfect time. It is never ahead of time, nor does it run behind time. There is no daylight savings time to cause confusion. One day there was a need to stop to see a missionary. Because it was urgent, I called them to let them know of my arrival. Upon arriving, no one was home. I waited a while, still no show. I drove around looking for them, no find. My schedule was tight that day, so it was necessary to leave. Driving toward the nearest town, wondering how to be able to see the missionaries, I had to stop at a red light. Looking out the window, there were the missionaries stopped across from me. I was able to get their attention and they pulled over. They had received an emergency call to the hospital and were trying to get home to meet with me. We had lunch together and took care of the business at hand, thus enabling me to make it to the next assignment on time. You see, I had need of patience and God's clock was keeping perfect time.

There is much to learn about God's love and how many times I have been placed in a position to learn a bit more about that great love. Learning to love the unlovely is a biggie! Just about every place, there is that unlovely person that needs love, God's love. One of those was an elderly lady who spent most of her time in the local tavern. She was drunk more than she was sober. Often she would pass out before she could make it home. One day we found her in the irrigation ditch in front of her house. It was fortunate for her that it was not the day the water came through. She had passed out and it was cold. We called for help and she was taken to the hospital. When she sobered up and realized where she was, she was terribly upset and gave the hospital a bad time.

She was finally sent home in spite of the fact she was very ill with pneumonia. We checked on her daily and did what we could to help her through very rough circumstances. It wasn't long till she was up and making her trips to the tavern again. At Christmas time, my partner had gone home to be with her mother for the holidays, leaving me there to keep things going at the church. Meanwhile the Lord had started a work in my heart and I realized that

God's love was the only way that very unlovely woman could be reached for Him. So she would become my Christmas project. Praying much, I fixed a big dinner and made a huge package filled with all kinds of goodies that she could use and enjoy. Arriving at her house, I had to knock on her door several times. Soon a gruff voice yelled out, "Come in, the door is open!" You wouldn't believe the trash, beer cans, and garbage that I had to wade through. There she was, stretched out across the bed. "What do you want?" she blurted out. I reminded her that it was Christmas day and I had brought her dinner and some goodies. She began to cry, because she was so overwhelmed. Before leaving that day, I was able to share God's love with her. She was so overwhelmed to receive all of this. I left the plan of salvation with her and she had much to think about that Christmas day. The seed had been planted and I was learning what God's love was all about!

While traveling, it seemed that many times I encountered some very negative circumstances. That was beginning to bother me, so my New Year's resolution was to learn how to rejoice in all situations. I even bought a book about continual rejoicing, thinking that would help. The book was lost before it could be read! God had a better way of teaching me to rejoice in all things. It was a cold day in January and my field work was finished for the time being. All had gone well and there was much rejoicing that another little church would soon have a full time village missionary. There would be a few days before I needed to be back for their arrival, so decided to go over the mountain to visit with some other missionaries. The roads were clear, so I headed up the mountain. My little Volkswagen began to slide to the other side of the road, due to some black ice. Not daring to put on the brakes, I prayed! Every time a car would come toward me, I would be back in my own lane long enough for it to pass. Finally, my car turned and was headed for a steep cliff. Just as the car was about to go over the cliff, it stopped with the front end hanging over the edge. The first thought that came to my mind was that I wanted to learn how to rejoice. Here it was—lesson time while half way over the cliff! Yes, the rejoicing began! Shortly I heard a knock on my window. It was two policemen ready to help me out of the mess. They pulled me back onto the road. The first thing they asked me was why I had not tried to get out of the car. The reply was that I was too busy rejoicing and praising the Lord that my car had not gone over. They told me that staying in the car was an excellent idea, because the movement would have sent the car plunging over the embankment. The engine was in the back of that little car so the weight had helped to lodge it in the snow bank. Many lessons were learned as I traveled upon numerous high places that year.

I had just arrived to open a closed church. There were enough interested people to come and help clean out the building. The mice had taken over, but it was soon all cleaned out. We purchased some Sunday school supplies and were very excited about that first Sunday. We were not disappointed because we had a full house that morning! The next Saturday, we went over to make sure everything was in order for the service the following morning. The Sunday school supplies, such as pencils and crayons had vanished! We checked all over and could not find a trace of them. So we went out and bought some more. After church, I checked the supplies and all the new ones were there. The next Sunday, the supplies had disappeared again, so we began to investigate. Not a trace of any crayons! This went on for several weeks. The rainy season had come, revealing several leaks in the church roof. So a work day was called and some of the men had to go up in the attic to fix the leaks. There they found a nest of pack rats, with the supplies that had disappeared. We spent the rest of that day cleaning the whole attic.

At this same little church, one Sunday I noticed, as I was giving the message, the congregation had strange expressions on their faces. I thought I must have said something wrong, but tried to act like all was fine. After all was said and done, they told me a little mouse was running around on the platform all the time I was speaking and had come very close to my feet a few times. We all learned some lessons in self control that day! A mouse trap was promptly set and that ended the "church mouse" episode.

I was blessed with an excellent sense of humor, but also needed to learn self-control. One Sunday as I was reading the Scripture lesson, a young lady burst into the church to get her mother, who was not supposed to stay for the worship service, just for Sunday school. I tried not to be distracted and continued to read. As the two of them went down the aisle, arguing out loud, the mother gave each one sitting on the aisle a pat on the head. Her rough hand had snagged a fine hair net off a lady's head, flipped it up in the air, and sent it onto the head of a bald headed man who was sitting in the row behind her! She continued on, still patting each person's head, while I continued reading. The congregation showed unusual self control till after the service, when everyone's sense of humor let loose!

Another time a little boy and his sister were sitting alone on the front pew during the service. The parents were not there and the boy started pestering his little sister. After taking all she could, she bit him fiercely on his arm. What a scream pierced the building! Once again, self-control had to be exercised. My co-worker was finally able to get them settled down as the service continued.

At another place, there was no church building and we were having our first meetings in a community building. There were folding chairs and a darling small boy, all dressed up in his Sunday-go-to-meeting clothes, was sitting right on the front row. Since it was his first Sunday to come to church, he was all ears. He sat with his feet propped on the rung of the chair, his elbows on his knees, and his hands holding up his head. He was deep in thought, taking in all that was happening. All of a sudden, his feet slipped off the chair rung and he landed on his stomach right in front of me! He promptly jumped up, brushed himself off, and perched himself on the chair again in the same position, just as if nothing ever happened! A lesson in restraint was taking place. There were countless lessons to be learned which would produce the fruit of the Spirit within me. A part of making my feet like hinds' feet was learning to make every incident count for the Lord—even the unexpected!

I had an appointment to get my hair permed, in a town where there had been a severe earthquake just the day before. A lot of damage had been done. There was no assurance that I could even get to the beauty shop. Upon arriving, I found the operator well shaken, wanting to share all her fears. Time was well spent in sharing with her about the One Whom I knew could give her peace. She was given a Stonecroft Life Publications booklet. Since she observed that I needed a haircut, an appointment was made for that later. Arriving the next week for the haircut, she met me at the door, asking for some more of those booklets. She had many friends who needed them, too. Once again, I was reminded of the power of God's Word. It is always fitting to share His Word. *"Preach the Word; be diligent in season, out of season." II Timothy 4:2 KJV "A word spoken in due season, how good it is!"* Proverbs 15:23 KJV

I was asked to speak at a baccalaureate service in one community, as well as to take part in the graduation. Participating in such occasions always gave me the opportunity to give each graduate a Stonecroft Life Publications booklet. When I arrived for the graduation, a young girl came rushing up to me with tears rolling down her cheeks and gave me a big hug. She finally pulled herself together enough to tell me her story. She had attended the baccalaureate service with the intention of going down to the river afterwards to commit suicide. When she got there, she decided to sit down on a rock first and read the little booklet I had given her. While reading it she realized that she had a reason to live, and prayed to receive the Lord Jesus as her Savior, right then and there! She was so thrilled and thankful for that booklet! It was hard for me to keep the tears from flowing! What a lesson I had learned! "*The steps of a [good] man are directed and established of the Lord, when He delights in his way [and He busies Himself with his every step.] Though he fall, he shall not be cast down, for the Lord grasps his hand in support and upholds him.*" Psalm 37:24 AMP

One Sunday I was invited to go home with a family for dinner. The mother was busy fixing a nice chicken dinner. The table was set and everything looked so good, until live chickens came into the house. One of the youngsters had left the door open for them. They were all over—on the table, the food, and everything else. She told the children to chase the chickens off. The footprints in the mashed potatoes did not seem to bother her! After the blessing was asked on the food, they served me first! Not wanting to hurt their feelings, I breathed a quick prayer that God would keep the food down and protect me from any bad results. God does answer prayer!

Yes, there are many lessons to be learned as we walk upon the high, steep places of trials, suffering, and responsibility. He is always there to grasp my hand and support me. I must just keep looking unto Jesus for His perfect will, which concerns me.

CHAPTER 10

Blessings Enjoyed While Walking in High Places

The Lord's blessings, that have been my privilege to experience while walking in high places, have never ceased to amaze me. There is no way to communicate all, but allow me to share a few of them.

During Bible college days, I had to work my way through. There was a need for five cents (along with my student pass for reduced rates) to ride the bus across town to my job. One day I discovered I did not have a nickel to my name. But I started for the bus stop any way, praying hard along the way. Arriving there, I looked down to find a nickel lying on the ground at my feet! I picked it up, got on the bus, and sat down. Just then a frightening thought entered my mind—How was I to get back home? Philippians 4:19 came to mind, *"But my God shall supply all your need according to his riches in glory by Christ Jesus."* KJV When I arrived at work, one of the teachers asked me if I would like a ride back to the college after school, because that day she would be going that way. Arriving back at the college, I decided to check my mail box. Guess what? There was a letter with ten dollars in it, providing quite a few more bus fares!

My partner, that I had on my first assignment, usually went home for Christmas. One of the church members asked me if I were going home for the holidays. I shared with him that IF God would work it out for Jean's mother to come and spend that period of time with her, IF God supplied the money for my bus ticket, and IF God would give me a verse of encouragement from His word that I should go, then I would go. Jean assured me that her mother would never come to spend Christmas with her. She was positive about that! The church member, a new Christian, who had asked me if I were going home, exclaimed, "You surely make it hard for God!" I replied, "That's the only way I can go home." When Jean received her weekly letter from her mother she was absolutely stunned! Her mother had informed her that she had been thinking that it would be fun to come spend Christmas with her that year! Request number one answered! God was at work because a few days later, I received a letter, with a check for the exact amount that was needed for a bus ticket to go home and return! Request number two on my list answered! Now for a verse of scripture to top it off! It was our custom to take a promise card from our promise box and read it before we asked the blessing at meal time. I took my promise and it said, *"Go home to thy friends, and tell them what great things the Lord hath done for thee, and hath had compassion on thee."* Mark 5:19b KJV It was wonderful to see God's will made so very clear, and a young Christian's faith growing along with that of the young missionaries.

There is always blessings in seeing the precious ways that God manifests His love to me. Being on a new field and seeing many children receiving Christ as their Lord and Savior and seeing their spiritual growth was overwhelming at times! On this particular day, which was my birthday, there came a knock on my door. Opening the door, there stood several of these new Christian children, laughing and having a big surprise for my special day. One of the older ones had baked a cake for me. Each one had a package wrapped (after a fashion) in newspaper—with even a bow on some! They were so anxious for me to open each gift!

They had searched their homes, looking for something to give. Some of the articles were slightly used, but, oh, so special in their eyes—and mine! Those darling children had worked all day on this surprise for me. The tears still come as I think of them. None of them had come from wealthy homes, but they had shared with me in their poverty! How blessed I was to have a birthday I shall never forget!

Sharing at a missionary conference in one of the Bible colleges, my heart was overwhelmed to find twenty-five of their students were from our little village mission churches. That made for a precious time of fellowship!

In one community a lady came to visit her friend. She finally consented to come to church with her. After services, we invited her over to the parsonage to talk over a cup of coffee. We discovered that she was a trapeze artist for a huge circus. Being extremely troubled and tired, she had come for some much needed rest, as well as hoping to get some of her problems solved. It did not take long for her to turn to Christ when she realized that He alone could help her solve all her problems. After she committed her life and heart to the Lord Jesus, she could hardly wait to call her husband to tell him what she had done. He was so pleased and we all rejoiced greatly that night!

It was time for camp and there were twenty-one young people signed up for camp. Some had never been to a camp of any sort, while others had never been to a church camp. A new experience was in store for all of them. We were ecstatic to see every camper, except two, make decisions to receive Christ as their personal Savior and follow Him in their lives. When we returned home we had a camp echoes service we shall never forget. The teenagers had complete charge of the service. Each one gave a personal testimony of how God had done a work in his or her heart. When they were finished, we allowed the adults to comment, if they so desired. Several of them stood, with tears streaming down their faces, to tell how God had spoken to their hearts in this service. Others were so touched that they could not speak. One man who had not been to church for over twenty years had come, just to see what the teenagers had to say. God spoke to his heart and he took his stand for Christ that night. A marvelous change took place in his life! He started coming to church every Sunday and the whole community talked about the change in him!

While visiting in a home one day, the lady said, "My friend and I have prayed for eight years asking God to send Christian leadership to our community. At last, God has answered our prayers!" My heart was blessed to think of having been a part in seeing prayers answered. These two ladies proved to be a blessing to me.

It is always a treat to work with children. One Sunday while teaching my Sunday school class, I asked, "Why did Jesus have to die?" A little girl replied, "Because He was getting old." It was a real blessing to be able to tell these children that Jesus had to die to take away our sins. That's how much He loved us all. *"For God so loved the world, that He gave His only begotten Son, that whosoever believeth in Him should not perish, but have everlasting life."* John 3:16 KJV There was a lively discussion that day answering their many questions. That was the very first time that little girl had ever heard about Jesus!

While on the road doing field work, I never knew what situation might be found. Once there was an area with five villages, with no witness for the gospel. Nearly three hundred and fifty families lived in this area, with one closed church. Marvelous was the blessing to see two village missionaries placed there.

It seems that the people in the rural areas are so open, anxious, and thrilled to have Christian leadership. They will not let distance keep them out of church. One lady would walk five miles to be in church! Another girl would walk eight miles through the woods in order to catch a ride to Sunday school and church. She would often bring her two younger sisters with her. One day she encountered a big black bear. Picking up a stick, she threw it at the bear, screaming at the top of her lungs at the same time. The bear ran off in another direction. Now she laughs as she tells, "I think I made better time to church that day!"

It is always a pleasure and a delight to participate in a missionary conference! How enjoyable to be with missionaries from all over the world. At one of these conferences, I noticed a young girl with an unusually troubled countenance. I smiled at her and spoke, then went on my way down the street to have some lunch and immediately heard someone running behind me. That troubled young girl caught up with me and began to tell me all about her problems. She was a new Christian, but her parents were not Christians and were not happy with her because she was. They were opposing her in every way, so she had just now run away from home. I encouraged her to call her parents right away so they would not worry about her. I gave her some Bible verses written on cards to encourage her to do the right thing and assured her of my prayers. The next day, we unexpectedly met at the elevator. As she ran to me with open arms and as she gave me a big hug, she told me that everything was going to be fine. She had called her folks and was on her way home. Later I received a letter from her that was filled with excitement. She said that her parents were going to church with her and were very pleased about her decision to become a Christian!

Remember that Sunday each spring and fall when we have to adjust our clocks an hour, called "Daylight Savings Time"? It seems that someone always comes to church an hour early—or an hour late. One of those Sundays, an eight year old boy with soggy pants arrived early. He had rushed to make it on time and the only pants he could find were still in the washing machine, clean but not yet dried. He had put them on and came to Sunday school so he wouldn't be late. His parents were still sleeping. We reminded him that he was an hour early and so would have time to run home and dry his pants. So he did and came back an hour later with dry pants, and a big smile. I shall never forget that little boy, a new Christian, who was so eager to come to Sunday school.

In one community, the Christians were so burdened for the lost people in their vicinity that they formed prayer groups to pray for the unsaved. For many weeks we had these prayer groups going in preparation for our evangelistic meetings. One of our village missionaries was to come and speak for a week of special meetings. God blessed that week with seventy-five decisions to receive Christ, for assurance and dedication. After our youth night when fifty young people went forward to make their decision for Christ, a teacher remarked, "I never thought I would see this happen in our community!" Earlier that evening we had put on a taco feed at the parsonage, where all of the junior and senior high school students were invited. Fifty-eight came for the tacos and one hundred and thirteen people came for that evening service.

Another great blessing enjoyed was one Sunday when opportunity was given to receive Christ, a certain men responded. The people were shocked, but thrilled. Everyone thought he was a Christian because he had donated the church property, as well as helped to build the building itself. He seldom ever missed a service. This particular Sunday was communion Sunday. The scripture in I Corinthians 11:28 says, *"But let a man examine himself...."* KJV God spoke to his heart and he realized he had all the marks outwardly of a Christian, but there had never been an inward change. So he asked Jesus to forgive him of all his sins and come into his heart to make that change—a day of victory he will never forget!

Each time this portable missionary had the privilege of going into a community to a church without leadership, she was on cloud nine, because the church doors would be opened once again! One tiny church had waited twelve years to have their doors opened. They were so excited that they worked hard to get ready for the new missionary family! The parsonage was in such bad shape they almost had to rebuild it. Did it ever look nice when the last bit of paint was finished! The kitchen shelves were stocked with food and one family was about to butcher, so a supply of meat was promised, too. The reception was overwhelming.

One day after a children's class, a little first grader asked if she could ask Jesus into her heart And that day, she did! She was so wound up, the next week she came bringing a friend with her. She, too, wanted to become a Christian. In her simple child-like faith, she received Christ as her personal Savior. Another little girl shared how she asked Jesus into her heart. We had seen a big difference in her actions, so we knew it was really true.

It was spring time and there was a special youth camp. We were thrilled to have twelve young people going from our community. We were even more thrilled to bring home twelve young people—all new Christians! One of the girls had picked up bottles along the road and sold them so she would have money to pay her way. The first night at camp, she found Jesus as her Savior. Monday at school, one of the new Christians bowed her head to ask the blessing on her lunch. Two other girls noticed her and came over to question her about it. She was pleased to share her testimony with them. They both decided they wanted to become Christians too! So right then and there, they took that big step!

Another time, at a Wednesday night prayer meeting, the group became burdened for a man in the community. His wife and children were at that meeting, who had shared the burden with us. Everyone prayed and committed this request to God. When they returned home afterward, he told how he had been out driving around while they were praying. He had become so under conviction of his sins that he just had to pull over to the side of the road and call out to God. He became a new creature in Christ Jesus. II Corinthians 5:17 KJV states that, "*Therefore if any man be in Christ, he is a new creation; old things are passed away; behold, all things become new.*" The next week, he was in prayer meeting to share his testimony. He also prayed out loud for the first time ever. What a joy and blessing to see this family happy and complete in the Lord!

One unforgettable Easter Sunday morning, our children's choir marched up on the platform to sing. Their mothers had helped to make the little robes for them from white sheets. Big red bows accented the cute little Peter Pan collars. It was all I could do to hold back the tears. Not because the singing was so heavenly, because most of them could not carry a tune in a bucket, but because we had the joy of seeing eight of these darling children come to know the Lord as their Savior. They were singing right from their hearts because they loved the Lord Jesus so much!

In another community, it was absolutely thrilling to see twenty people enrolled in a Scripture memorization course. Young and old alike would stay after services on Sunday to say the verses they had learned to someone else. "*Thy word have I hidden in mine heart, that I might not sin against thee.*" *Psalm 119:11* KJV When we tuck God's Word away in our hearts, it is always there to comfort us and help us. The verses I learned as a child are still a blessing and help to me.

In a ladies' Bible class and prayer meeting, we were all just sharing God's blessings in our lives, when one lady broke down and started to cry. She told of her need for God and right then and there opened her heart to Him. Great thanksgiving was raised to the Lord for all the blessings, especially for this new Christian!

One Sunday, two new families appeared in church. Everyone was elated to have them there, for they had taken time out of their skiing vacation to attend church. The next week, the ski lift broke while they were going up, leaving them stranded high up and in a very dangerous position. While hanging in mid air, the Sunday message kept coming to mind. They talked about it and applied God's Word to their own hearts. Before long the lift was repaired and took them on their way. As they shared this incident with us the following Sunday, they related how thankful they were to have been in church to hear that message. It was just what they had needed that eventful week.

A Girl Scout camp was fairly near in one community and the camp director called to ask if it would be all right to bring the whole camp to our church for the next two Sundays. Of course, I was pleased. It was so thrilling to have fifty girl scouts in our worship service. They filled up half the church so we had a full house those Sundays!

The blessings enjoyed while walking in high places continue on and on. I am still having a life filled with His strength and joy. I think of the many miles this portable missionary has traveled with God's protection and the many needs He has supplied. How can I keep from praising Him?

When Betty and I came to California, we rented a big house to be used for Bibles studies, prayer coffees, and having house guests. Having been a house guest in so many different homes, so many times, I just wanted to be "on the other side" of the fence (so to speak). It was always so special to stay in other homes and enjoy their gracious hospitality, where the welcome mat was always out. I remember one place when the hostess took me to the room I was to occupy and she informed me that, "This time your room is different. We put in new furniture, because those of you who travel need a good bed so you can get your rest." She never let me leave her home without a supply of goodies to enjoy along the way.

Another special home I shall never forget was always open to me. She even allowed me to store things at her house, as it was in a location that I drove through frequently. Not only was she a lovely hostess, but she would always pack a lunch for me when I left. Many times there would be a verse of scripture tucked in the lunch. That was a real blessing as I traveled on my way. So having house guests was a special treat for us.

After renting for several years, we decided to buy our own home. Praying much about it, God led us to a darling house. It was so much fun fixing it up! We had a lot of activity there—Bible studies, childrens' classes, prayer meetings, board meetings for our local Christian Women's Club, even some fun parties, and were privileged to entertain numerous house guests. Once again, we enjoyed God's blessings beyond words!

Betty continued to work for a few more years after I retired, so we also had the teachers to come for lunch and her first graders walked over on field trips. I thoroughly enjoyed all the events.

BREAKING NEWS!!!

The past six years of my retirement have meant more high places of trouble, suffering and responsibility. We moved and lived in three different towns, which proved to be God's perfect will for us. The suffering part came with cataract and glaucoma surgery, quadruple by-pass heart surgery, and carotid artery surgery. Quite an organ recital, huh? But that is not the end, because I developed eye lid problems which made me functionally blind (although I have almost perfect vision). Something went wrong with the muscles, so the only way for me to see was to hold up my eye lids with my fingers. What a nightmare!

Writing this book has been a time consuming process, under these circumstances. Our last move brought us where there are some excellent doctors. Just as this book is being finished, I have had surgery on my eye lids, enabling me to open them without the use of my fingers. How great that the Master Physician not only cares about making me have hinds' feet, but also is concerned for my eyes that I may see. My life has been enriched with innumerable physical and spiritual blessings as a result of all these high places of trouble, suffering, and responsibility.

CHAPTER 11

Church Bells Are Ringing

Zelma, ringing the church bell.

Church bells have always held a fascination for me. I love to hear them and always wanted to ring a church bell. That desire was fulfilled when I arrived on my first assignment in rural America. What an excitement for me! The following pictures represent just a few of the rural churches that I have had a part in helping to keep the doors open. It was fun ringing the bell, calling the whole community to worship!

Elk River, ID

Phillipsburg, MT

Fernwood, ID

Fairveiw, OR

Bellevue, WA

Charlos Heights, MT

Starbuck, WA

Sierraville, CA

Star, CO

Logan, OR

The Village

It was just a little village
Tucked away from out of sight,
And it had some precious souls
Without the gospel light.

God looked down with compassion
And found a willing soul,
Who went to that little village
And there the gospel told.

Today that little village
Has a light house of its own,
And people come from far and near
To worship and make Him known.

Let us pray for the many villages
Who still are waiting out there,
May they too have a missionary
Who will come to them and share.

Written by Zelma for all our dear village missionaries and their families.

My Life Verse

God gave me two very special verses when I was a teenager and I have claimed them as my life verses.

"Wherefore, seeing we also are
compassed about with so great
a cloud of witnesses, let us lay
aside every weight, and the sin
which doth so easily beset us, and
let us run with patience
the race that is set before us,
Looking unto Jesus, the author and
finisher of our faith, who
for the joy that was set before him
endured the cross,
despising the shame, and is set
down at the right hand of the
throne of God."
Hebrews 12:1,2 KJV

Conclusion

The Lord God has been, and still is, my personal bravery and my invincible army. He continues to make my feet like hinds' feet and keeps me walking, not standing still in terror, but walking, and making spiritual progress upon my high places of trouble, suffering, and responsibility. He is not finished yet. I am so thankful for a living God who is so very real to me. He is so faithful and has promised to never leave me nor forsake me. He hasn't tossed me on the junk heap, but continues to work with me day after day. My prayer is that He will perfect in me what He has started. *"Being confident of this very thing, that he who began a good work in you will perform it until the day of Jesus Christ."* Philippians 1:6 KJV He will not give up on me!

Being a retired missionary does not mean the high places are any easier. They seem to come more frequently. But God is still in charge and I praise Him for strength!

I would not feel my story would be complete without inviting you, dear friend, to let this same God make your feet like hinds' feet. You will never regret taking that big first step. I surely did not! He has not and never will fail me, nor will He disappoint you.

> *"Then spoke Jesus again unto them saying, I am the Light of the world; he that followeth me shall not walk in darkness, but shall have the light of*

life." John 8:12 KJV "But as many as received him, to them gave he the power to become the (children) of God, even to them that believe on his name." John 1:12 KJV

It is an act of faith—just a matter of recognizing that you are a sinner. *"For all have sinned, and come short of the glory of God."* Romans 3:23 KJV No matter how good we are, we are all sinners. We must confess our sins to God and ask Him to forgive us. We must place our faith in Jesus Christ, who died on the cross for us. The next step is to ask the Lord Jesus to come into our lives and take control. Then comes the peace and joy that He alone can give.

If you would like to take that big step, it is so simple. Just pray from your heart something like this:

"Dear Lord Jesus,
I believe You are God's Son, who died for my sins. Please, forgive my sins and come into my life. I am turning from my old ways and will follow You completely. Please be my Leader and take control of my life. Thank you for the Gift of eternal life and Thank you that the Holy Spirit now lives in me.

In Jesus' name,
Amen.